Among the
Dying Violets

Novels by Barb Shadow

A Step Into Darkness

Shifting to Black

Invitation to Darkness

Among the Dying Violets

Barb Shadow

Copyright © 2020 Barb Shadow

All rights reserved.

ISBN: 978-0-9998374-3-6

Cover Designer: Ivano Lago

All rights reserved. No part of this publication may be reproduced, distributed, or transmitted in any form by any means, including photocopying, recording, or other electronic methods without the prior written permission of the author, except in the case of brief quotations embodied in reviews and certain other noncommercial uses permitted by copyright law. For permission requests, write to the author at barbshadowwrites@gmail.com.

From the Shadows Publishing
Forestburgh, New York

To those I love

We joke about the darker things
And laugh with an irreverence
That is remarkably healing

Any resemblance
To persons living or dead
May be purely coincidental
But if you recognize yourself
Within these pages
Don't blame me

Enjoy your purgatory

Enter at Your Own Risk

None of this makes sense
No happy little poems
Tied together by theme
Put into a special little book
Under someone's pillow
No screaming heartache
Or love sonnets
Pain between pressed flowers
Mine are an odd conglomeration
Falling short of chest beating
Gut wrenching
Spoken word poetry
I've lived the drama
But the words are quiet
And silence
Is scary

My Soul Exposed

I showed you my poems last night
I should have been drunk
Or at least had a glass of wine in hand
Rosy cheeks and a light head
Something on which to blame
My indiscretion
I read them to you
One by one
Even the worst ones
And you said,
"You were going to make me wait
Until you were dead to read these???
Don't Emily Dickinson me."
And we smiled and laughed
Mine in nervous expectation
Desperate to share them with you
And terrified
And you said they were good
They were *POETRY*
And I said no…
They are a struggle
Of inadequate words
A broken pen
A soul constrained
I think I need a drink

Childhood Memories

There should be some things
There should be

Like ribbon candy and petit fours
And black and white photos with bent corners
Marvel the Mustang and red metal dump trucks

Chocolates with caramel centers
Parades on TV while searching for the puzzle piece with a little green
and just some yellow
On the side

Spinning spaceships and gyroscopes
Calculators with just four functions
And file cabinet box-tunnels with the cat

Fluffy robes and slippers
A dog's aching stomach from stolen stollen
Staring at the grey blue sky with snow clouds forming

Silent echoes of Christmas past
You have moved to memory
And winter comes too fast

There should be more time
There should be

My Grandpa

I remember my grandpa's house
Mostly after he was gone
The long walk up the side steps
Beside the rose bush
To the enclosed porch
That reeked of cat food
And cardboard boxes
The front porch a maze
Of twine-tied newspaper stacks
And dingy wicker furniture

We moved through the kitchen
And I ran my hand along
The 1950's appliances
Or they could have been forever older
Memories from a child's mind
They were so much larger then
We walked to the living room
Dark
I don't think there were windows
Although there must have been
Bits of sunlight through pulled drapes
Afghans on sofa backs
A coffee table
With aged photographs
Postcards
And love letters
Under glass
TV trays for snacks
And Grandpa's recliner
Pots of violets
A carpet that could've been velvet
But must not have been
I remember the worn spots

Aunts and Uncles
Cousins
Gatherings with dinner-party voices
Holidays and celebrations
Grandma brought me ginger ale
In a small green glass
To look like the drinks the adults had
I sat one afternoon on the old sofa
Cutting pictures out of Christmas cards
And we never went upstairs

Grandpa sat in his chair
In the corner
I'd climb onto his lap
A black and white television nearby
Johnny Carson in the background
Or maybe just talk of Carson
I was too young to be up that late

I remember Grandpa
Taking me to school one morning
Although I don't know why
I might have been in Kindergarten
Or first grade
And we rode in his Jeep
My feet dangling above the floor
With the hole
I watched the ground moving beneath us
Fascinated and a little nervous
But not
Because Grandpa was there
And the hole was too small
To slip through

Barb Shadow

The last time I saw him
I was on the street
Beside Mom's car
Next to a stone building
And someone told me to look up
It might have been Mom
Maybe Dad
And through a window a few stories above
An arm waved
My Grandpa's arm
I smiled
Waved back
Children weren't allowed
In the hospital
But I should have been
Or maybe it's better
That I wasn't
And my last memory
Is a loving wave
Rather than my grandpa's face
Knowing he wouldn't be going home
To sit in his chair
And watch late night television
Again

When I was Young, I Played Outside

When I was young, I played outside
Reveled in the beauty of the grass and trees
The clean, crisp morning air

I knocked on doors
Called out friends
And built forts among the bushes
We swept pine needles
For a smooth dirt floor
And drank from hoses

We tried to climb the rough-barked trees
Got sticky hands from sap
And told each other stories
We popped tar bubbles on the road
In old, holey sneakers
And dreamed of the future
While staring at clouds
On our backs in the field

We crushed stones into powder
To make paint
And carried in groceries
When our mothers yelled
Bologna sandwiches
And hide and seek games in my basement
When the sun got too hot

We scraped knees and skinned elbows
When our Big Wheels overturned
After flying down the hill
Holding our feet out
While the pedals spun free

Barb Shadow

We scooped up polliwogs
And marveled at salamanders
Ran fingers over wooly bears
To turn them into fuzzy wheels
As crayfish hid in streams
We skipped rocks across the lake

We rode our bikes
Took half-mile walks
To the country store
For chips and soda
The only store in town
A creaky wooden floor
Small glass counter
With box fans whirring
The owner ready to sell fireballs
Candy necklaces
Fishing poles
And worms

Dinners were hot dogs and hamburgers
Grilled over charcoal
Eaten at the picnic table
With the red peeling paint
Or inside with the lights off and fans going
We had no a/c
It was hot, it was good
It was summer

We'd play outside till the streetlight came on
And rush to get home
Everyone scattering
Tired and happy
Excited for what adventures
The next day would bring

When I was young, I played outside
But the world is different now
Technology has taken over
And my heart goes out to little ones
Who are lost in devices
Instead of carefree summer days

Hidden

There is a skull
Filled with potpourri
On my night table
And a sign that reads
"Home sweet haunted home"
On the living room wall
Skeletons are literally
In my closet
Waiting for Halloween display
But there are also ones
Who rattle their bones
When strangers walk by
Aching to let their secrets loose
And when I whisper
"Shhh"
They settle in for a while longer
But I don't know how long
They can be restrained

My Father

I get it now, Dad
I get it
I understand
Even though you're three years gone

I found the letters
In Grandpa's trunk
That stood so long
In the garage
Musty and dirty

After all the years
Of barely tolerating
Your presence
Till you were old
And mellowing
I realize
You didn't know how to love
To show you cared
To be a parent

Something led me
To those letters
I think it was Grandpa's spirit
Trying to make amends
Explain why his son
Had been so difficult
As a father
Maybe it was his apology
To you
To us

He wrote to Grandma

Barb Shadow

Your step-mom to be
At the time
And told her of his pain
Heartache
Loss of faith
That had been his core
And so essential to his being
When his Beatrice passed away
How lost he had been
And if it weren't for his boys
He would have joined her
And I've pieced it all together

Grandpa was a broken man
And blamed you
Instead of the love of his life's
Damaged heart
He blamed your fever
For being the final blow
That let Death take her
But couldn't separate the boy
From the illness
You didn't know
And were too young
To understand his resentment

We bungled through my childhood
You more interested in your
Linotype, photography
Outcrops, camping
Genealogy, electronics
Ham radio
I sat in the car
While you chipped at rocks

Wandered cemeteries
Looking for long lost relatives
Searching for a thread to the past
Someone who cared
I wander them now
But seeking ghosts
Same thing, almost

We lived separate lives
In the same house
You tried, I think
The Christmas you gave me red magnets
One year a red frisbee
A skillet
You tried to bridge the divide
At scattered moments
But when you yelled at my sister
Berated our grandmother
Beat the dog
It broke something
Within us

As you aged
I think Grandpa needed to show me
Needed to let us know
Why you were so tortured
His regret
Led to our understanding
And forgiveness of his son
And maybe someday
It will lead to yours
Of him

Unspoken

We sat together
In the kitchen
Mom and I
Making quiet conversation
As daylight faded
Into evening
Empty coffee cups
On the crumb littered tablecloth
A pause

"So, tell me," she said,
"What do crows mean?"

A dull black bird had landed
On the electric lines
And stared
Through her picture window
Mom noted his features
Met his gaze
And thought it strange
To be the object
Of his attention

Never one for superstitions
Omens
Or folklore
But recognizing her own
Mortality
She pondered the creature
Who returned each day
And when she walked
From room to room
Followed
Tree to fence

"They mean death, don't they?"
She tried to pass it off
Indifferent
Only curious to know
What my spiritual
And paranormal background
Would say
Not that she believed in it

I shrugged
Said they could mean
Many things
And grabbed my phone
To look up
A definitive answer
But in actuality
Avoiding the question
Blaming bad internet
No cell reception
I'd research it
When I got home
And let her know
tomorrow

In our hearts
We both knew
What crows could mean
And never spoke of it
Again

Death

He came at the wrong time
Without consultation or question
No, "Would this fit into your schedule?"
Not even, "Do you mind?"
Without a wave of his hand
Or backwards glance
Faceless
Nameless
We give him too much
This soul stealer personified
In our meekest moments
We tremble
Reach out
To touch a cloak
That isn't there
A last breath on parted lips
A cycle completed
Never at the right time

The birch trees that I loved so much
Are gone
And the landscape of my life has changed

Moms Don't Die

I don't know what you're talking about
Because moms don't die
Moms are amazing things
And indestructible
Bee stings and skinned knees
Tear-stained dirty summer faces
Melt into the comfort
Of a mother's arms
It's all okay
It will always be okay
Because moms don't die
I made mistakes as all teens do
But always with a home
And a mom
Who loved me regardless
And was my safety net when the world
Set me on a tightrope
I could walk the precarious walk
Fearful but steady
Mom was there
Knowing in her heart that I could do it
Even when I didn't
I would make it
I could make it
With Mom watching along the way
Letting me know that
It would always be okay
I was smart and strong
And she would always be with me
Because moms don't die
When I found that inner confidence
Mom smiled and was proud that I had discovered
What she had always known
And we would talk

At some point in our lives
We became confidants
And friends
I depended on her quiet strength
And, later, she on mine
For more than just the little things
But that is the way of life sometimes
And time runs out
And moms do die
But when I hit the hard times,
I feel her at my shoulder, looking on
And saying, "You've got this."
And I do

Mom

Death crept in at night
Warning the shadows
To wait in the fringe areas
A familiar darkness
Anticipated
But not truly desired

Were there shadows watching
as Death touched you
setting aside your pain
letting you make
the final decision
of this life?

He was only the bridge
Taking your hand
As your soul let go
And placing it in
Your father's
mother's

A stillness as our hearts break
A smile as you understand
Until we meet again

I Passed the Cemetery Today

I worry
My car will get stuck
In the rain-filled ruts
And that it's already too chilly
To stay for long
And I know
You aren't really there
Just a rotting body
Under the ground
I walk the uneven grass
And when I touch the stones
They're so cold
And rough
Faded etchings
I come to touch
A quiet space
Of contemplation
A slight breeze
The sound of cars
On the highway
Another second ticks by
But your watch has stopped
Hasn't it

W

You cried
In Mom's bedroom
As we tried to wake her
My father in the hallway
Lost
Confused
When I called her name
Shook her
You said, "She's gone,"
And broke down
I called 911
Dealt with paramedics
The police
And Dad
You sat by her side
And wept
Unashamed
Let the medics calm you
As I turned on my heel
To meet the coroner
Make arrangements
And phone calls
You mourned her
As if she had been your own

I think it was the last
Genuine emotion
You had

Mom

I said I'd never go to the cemetery
You're not there
I know in my heart
You're over my shoulder
Keeping an eye on things
And yet I go
Clear away the cut grass
Make sure the little plastic cardinal
And school bell
Are standing upright
I touch the stone
And miss your voice
I allow the quiet sadness
To settle over me
The way twilight
Eases into night

The Changing of the Guard

Our matriarchy has ended
We have been thrown
Into splintered factions
Each caring for his own
Grasping threads
To the past

I try to keep scrambled eggs
On the griddle
With a spatula
Quickly scraping
And sliding tendrils
Back to the center
But it never works completely
Does it

Mom poured pancake batter
Kept sausage links rolling
So they wouldn't burn
Made tiny meatballs
For her lasagna
And kept us all together
Cinnamon-sugar toast memories
On snowy mornings

As I swing into the drive-thru at Dunkin
Coffee to go
A bagel with cream cheese
I miss her

I am the Bee

Between you and me, I am the bee.
The women in our family,
Every generation been and gone,
Have been.
I don't know how to fill these shoes,
If bees wear shoes,
But I will be remembered
When I am cold.
"She was the bee,"
They will think
Or offer up in teary tones.

When I ascended,
By chance or fate,
A rusty, dented crown
Was presented
As if covered
In a thousand jewels.
I tucked it inside my heart
And moved on
In disbelief
But when you are the bee
You do.

And, thirty years hence,
When teachers assign
To their students
In large, lofty voices
A dissertation
On the meaning of the bee,
And speculate, "Was she queen?"
In whispers with dark-roomed voices,
I will smile
And turn in my grave
To a more comfortable position.

Barb Shadow

Because,
Between you and me,
I am the bee.

Icicles

Mom's house had icicles
We watched them grow
Stalactites of melted roof-snow
We jumped to bat them
Off the gutters
Watch them shatter
Into shards
On the cement porch

Mom's house had icicles
That sparkled like diamonds
We'd break the longest ones
The cold drips numbing our tongues
Before we tossed them away
Into snowbanks

Mom's house had icicles
As old homes do
Where the heat leaks
And the drafts sneak in
I watch the snow fall
Through the windows
Of my living room
Cozy and warm
And miss the icicles
On Mom's house

My Star

We played your songs last night
Hits from the '40's
And I sang along
With the ones I could remember
That you used to sing
On long car rides

I felt you sit beside me
And I had to smile
Share with your granddaughter
That you were there
Singing along
Going through the motions
Of Catch a Falling Star
And Put it in Your Pocket
The same way you did
When I was a child

I cling to the times
I can sense you
Clear as day
Just behind my right shoulder
And hear your voice
In my mind, yet not

You never bought in
To my passion
For all things ghostly
I wonder what you think now
If you nod
And acknowledge
That I was onto something

Yet I am aware
That all the books in the world

My investigations
And research
Can't hold a candle
To what you are experiencing

Someday we'll be together once again
And have a long talk

When it's Me

What will you do when it's me?

Life's hard reality is death takes us all
And I can't even stay clear-eyed as I write these words

What will you do when it's me?

I'm not setting myself high on a pedestal
Crying to the heavens
Beating my breast
Exaggerating my own self-worth
But quietly letting my own heart break

When I cease to be in this world's form
I cannot comprehend
Cannot fathom
Leaving you to whatever next step awaits

What will you do when it's me?

Mom's Piano

Mom's piano is immortalized
In acrylic paint
On a small canvas
In my bedroom

A black baby grand

There is a warmth
In the tones
And they remind me
Of summers past
When I was young
And the sun shone
Through big picture windows
And dust rode on sunbeams

I would slide onto the bench
Open the fallboard
Expose the smooth keys
And pick out one-fingered tunes
While Mom read a library book
Or was off teaching summer school

She scrimped and saved
To purchase the instrument
So dearly loved
As we didn't have a lot of money then
Even our trips into town
Were measured
Combined
The grocery store
Laundromat
Dentist appointments
Making long Saturday mornings

Barb Shadow

Of errands
To save gas
But Mom saved
And upgraded
From the upright player piano
That was in the basement
Out of tune
With broken keys

Mom sat before
Her baby grand
Fingers poised
With passion flowing
And when she opened the lid
To free the strings
The house resonated
Beethoven
Tchaikovsky
Debussy
And Mozart
Mom's favorite
And mine
She'd play every show tune you could imagine
And sing along
She even played the Beatles
From time to time
To Mom, music was a beautiful expression
Of mathematics
And precision
The syncopation of ragtime
Fascinated her
She would play
For hours on end
And I remember when she brought home

Among the Dying Violets

A record titled "Music Minus One"
She would play the piano section
And be part of an orchestra
Vicariously living
Her Carnegie Hall dreams
While teaching paid the bills

We grew up around that piano
In the far end of the living room
In winter
And beside the front door
In summer
For a breeze
I took lessons on those keys
Never quite good enough
In my mind
Always in the shadow
Of the consummate musician
Who only wanted me to do my best
And share the joy
Of music

One day my cousin placed a glass
On the piano
To which my mother firmly stated,
"The piano is an instrument,
Not a piece of furniture,"
Which opened his eyes
With a newfound respect
And he removed his drink
He told me the story
Before her funeral
And said he never again
Rested anything on a piano

Barb Shadow

I had to empty her house
After her death
When Dad went to the nursing home
And I knew I had to sell the piano
We could carry Mom's music in our hearts
But none of us
Had space
For a baby grand
In our living rooms

The men came with straps
And a truck
Took the legs off the instrument
And slid it on its side
It will be refinished
Sold as used
No one knowing its history
Or the hours of happiness
It enabled

But

Mom's piano is immortalized
In acrylic paint
On a small canvas
In my bedroom
And I will keep it
In my heart
Forever

There is No Duct Tape

"Where's the duct tape?" I ask on a breezy April morning
Spring cleaning dust on my fingertips
Waiting to tie shut garbage bags of dreams
Papers, school assignments, dried out markers and old, ripped jeans

"There is none," he replies. I try the junk drawer
Pawing through paint brushes, screwdrivers
And measuring tape
Puncturing my fingers on tacks that haven't held up Christmas lights
In four months

There is none. I find sticky black electrical tape
And wrap loops around the plastic bag
Filled to bursting with worn out books
Used for tests and tossed aside
And smile at my ingenuity

I sit. Satisfied with my day
Yet undone, with more to dispose of
You are on the other half of the couch
Lost in television dreams
Instead of the voices of your children

There is no duct tape

I've Grown Used to the Wrong Things

You yelled too much today
Too long, too loud
I didn't even flinch
But the robins scattered
Taking with them
Spring

Are You Sorry?

I want an apology
    For the wounds you left
    That haven't healed
    And ache with suspicion

I didn't know
    How much my trust
    Bled out
    Until someone new
    Touched my heart
    And those nerves

    So raw and just below the surface

And Not the Only One

My favorite wine
Has your first name
How ironic
To brand
Your weapon of choice

You Never Could Understand

An absent father
Who made occasional appearances
Bearing gifts to appease
His guilt
Who never understood
Your resentment
When he put strangers above
His own family

A single mother who raised you
With strings attached
And payback
Taught you that money and looks
Were valued
And men were utilitarian
You were only as good
As the last thing you fixed
And the phone was silent
Until a lightbulb popped
Groceries needed carrying
Or the grass was too tall

A love-hate relationship
With one sister
Who showed you how
To stick a finger down your throat
Because being thin
Was more important
Than being healthy
Who would go for months
And later years
Without speaking to you
Until your mother begged you
To make up
Even when it wasn't your fault

Barb Shadow

An older sister
Who adored you
With a husband who became
Your closest friend
Until a miscommunication
Of which you were unaware
Caused them to cut you
Then me
Out of their lives
Because it was easier
Than discussion

They left you to flounder
Alone in the darkness
Until pain boiled to rage
And it ate you alive
The venom spewing
In every direction
Not just inward

And they rallied
When you died
Brought sandwiches
Hugs
And offers of
Anything we needed
But they had to have
A copy of the death certificate
To satisfy
Their morbid curiosity
And I'm sure the whispers
And gossip
Flew

You appreciated unconditional love
And loyalty
But were too broken
To return it
And never truly understood the concept
Anyway
It's hard to give
What you had never received

Bad Days

We had our good days
I don't remember them
Though the other times are perfectly clear
Your drunken tirades
And next morning regrets
Not being able to look me in the eye
Because you saw what you were becoming

You lost your children
When you forced your way into their rooms
Punched holes in the walls
Tried to impart your wisdom
By yelling insults in their faces
And reacting with spite
When they tuned you out

And when your middle child
Poured the rest of your beer down the drain
While you were sleeping off the night before
You found the presence of mind
To realize the path you were on
Yet still told her to never do that again

I played the mediator far too long
Tried to absorb the brunt of your ranting
Stayed awake until your breathing changed
So I knew we could safely sleep
And you'd be out until long after the sun came up

You didn't destroy your relationship
With your youngest
It's hard to wreck something
That never existed
He thrived regardless of the nights

You stood over him screaming
Letting me know
I wasn't worth dirt
And I knew as long as I kept my mouth shut
Your slurring would turn into
An alcohol sleep
And the tension would ease
For a little while

I can't count
The number of times you slept
On the floor
In your own vomit
And got up the next day
To clean up and hate yourself
But still blame me
For not helping you
When we both knew I couldn't

And I will forever think back
To the night you died
When you told your oldest child
That you hadn't been a good father
And didn't know how to fix it
Maybe something deep inside
Knew you were at the end
And couldn't make amends

Barb Shadow

I grew tired of walking on razor blades
to close the distance between us.

The Phoenix and the Bear

I dreamed of bears
For many years
And searched for meaning
In their motions
Walking through my nights
In strength
And confidence
I kept my distance
Respectful
Yet afraid
Not knowing if I should run
I dreamed of bears
It took time
To understand their message
Their embodiment
Of standing against hardship
And taking action
I should have grasped it sooner
I dreamed of bears
In times of difficulty
But that was our life
Wasn't it
I needed their inner strength
And fearlessness
In my daily life
With you
I dreamed of bears
And finally learned
To stand tall
And embrace the fire
In my soul

I live amid the phoenix and the bear

No More, Please

I'll never forget that morning
When the phone rang
And Dad asked when I'd be coming
Because he didn't think
You were breathing.
His Alzheimer's a shield to your death

    Coffin, pall bearers, flowers
        Minister, service, graveyard

I'll never forget that morning
I put the coffee on
And tried to wake you
But you were already cold
And 911 made me do CPR
Until the ambulance arrived

    Coffin, flowers, minister
        Service, crematory, silence

I'll never forget that morning
Another phone call
A message passed along
Dad's Alzheimer's had won
And his body would now
Rejoin his mind

    Coffin, pall bearers, flowers
        Minister, service, graveyard

The funeral director knows me
By first name now
And we've spent too much time
In mourning.

W

Your life was wrapped up
In a tight package
Within the two-week span
Of a school break
Alive
Dead
Back to routine
And a new normalcy
No one is indispensable
Life goes on
The sun comes up
And I can smile again

Not Yet Gone

It's been a year, some months,
And you're still around
Not in the dreamy, Hallmark card
Forever in my thoughts
Will always miss you way
Because I don't
You said you'd find a way
To make your presence known
If you went first
When I was picking out the blue shirt
For your funeral
And heard
I like black
I put the blue one down
The time for spite is gone
That was your game anyway
When I was folding clothes
In the bedroom
And the light flicked on
In the closet
I was sure
And when I heard
A man's voice
Say my name
In the hallway
I knew who it was
Time is moving on
And I hope you're happy where you are
Because I am happy here

Gone

Dead two years
And you had to hurt me
One last time
The letters she wrote
Tucked inside an old book
On our bookshelf
Waiting for the day
When I would paint
Rearrange
Make the room into my own
Take charge of my life
Without you
No, it didn't break my heart
It brought back
Yesterday's anger
Sent me into the pain
Of old arguments
Thirteen years melted
Into ten minutes
And I was mad
How dare you deny the relationship
I knew you had outside of us
How dare you
My trust rested on
The earthquake of you
A life of doubt
We outlasted you and her
And she missed your downward spiral
Missed you doubling down
on your drinking
and your growing darkness
But
truly
we died years before

Barb Shadow

Do not back me into a corner.
I'm armed with the truth and I'm not afraid to use it.

Let it Go

I am trying hard to take the high road
To leave behind old pain
But we round the bend each year
The cycle of birthdays and death-days
And you post again
Oblivious of the anger and resentment
The ache
It churns in me
I should just close my eyes
But something in me needs to see
Has to touch the nerve
He cultivated
And you reveled in
Both so selfish and dysfunctional
It's nice that you're with someone else now
And seem happy in your life
So please
Stop walking on my heart
In cleats

Barb Shadow

>
> Life is about
> Putting out fires
> When what you really want
> Is to burn bridges

W

As I flip through a stack of photographs
I see your face
Almost two years and you'd think I'd have recovered by now
I don't miss you
But it's like a punch to the gut that leaves a knot in my stomach
And mind
I stare at your face, trying to read something not written
Unfamiliar
As if looking at a stranger
And yet
Your ashes are still in my closet

Barb Shadow

It's Not Always Easy

I'm in heels
Dodging potholes
Uphill
In 105 degree
Summer heat
With no clouds
A burn settling into my shoulders
And mind
But I trudge on

I'll Never Know

Why

With the heavens laid out before us
Did you choose hell?

Why
Knowing dark clouds
Promised silver linings
Did you cave to storms?

Why
When you poured out your pain
Could you not heal the void
With my love?

Why
As you were shattering
And I tried to peace
Your shards together
Did you cut me?

Barb Shadow

Where do you find shelter from internal storms?

I have a phoenix tattooed on my wrist
It reminds me that I stand
On the other side of the chasm

Moving On

I stand by the cemetery gate
Trees swaying in the breeze
A break in the clouds
Rays of sun
Highlighting violets
Near an empty grave
I sigh
A faint smile on my lips
I don't mind
Burying our relationship
Without a stone
Without a plot
Just a wave good-bye
Which was more
Than you gave me

Changes

I am plagued by moments of melancholy
Interspersed with happiness
I'm trying to grasp
White knuckle grip
It's been so long
Without sun on my skin
You faded the outside world
To a dark storm cloud
Tried to fill me with fear
But now you're gone
And I have changed
To full-on phoenix
Regaining control
Exhilarated
Terrified
But I've got this
And there is no going back
I am fueled
Fed
recharged
By the challenge
Of living life
And touching the world
In a way that you
Could never have imagined

Poetry

Just doesn't work for me
I am the failed poet
But that doesn't mean
I haven't lived
Felt
Screamed
Cried
Loved
Or raked my fingernails
Down a back
In perfect orgasmic fashion
My words just fall short
Of their destination

My Fears
A work in progress

That I will never fall in love again
Never feel that anticipation
And desire
Heart skipping like a stone on water
Thrown with direction
Caution to the wind
Breath held to see how far it will go
Fingers crossed in excitement

That I will die
One day too soon
While my kids still need me
And I will feel them reaching for me
But they won't notice my arms around them
And I won't be able to fix it
Take care of things
Make it better

That I will run out of money
Before I run out of life
And my children will take on a burden
They don't deserve
And shouldn't feel necessary

That I will get Alzheimer's
Like Grandpa did
And lose all of you
Long before I'm gone
It rattles me

Cold Feet

My feet are cold
And slippers don't help
I stand in the doorway
Searching an overcast sky
Dull and grey
Tree branches swaying
As rain approaches
Or maybe snow
A time of self-reflection
Hands wrapped around
My coffee mug
I breathe in the steam
But my mood echoes the wind
As low pressure settles in
Happiness
Is on the horizon
But today, life's challenges taunt me
And answers are elusive
I take a deep breath
Exhale
Some well-needed sleep
Might refresh my perspective
But my feet are too cold

Is This All There Is?

Day to day
The bills paid
The cats fed
The sun rises
Goes down
I'm alone
Is this all there is?
It's all good
I'm okay
I wash my face
Put on a smile
And at the end of the day
Set it on the night table
When I climb into bed
To sleep

Ephemeral

I am mortal and it scares me
Death has been in my face
And his wagging finger
Has taken me aback
Mom gone and Dad
My husband
Four cats
My dog
In the last three and a half years
It's real now
More so than ever before
Not a concept
Or a grieving process
And I've realized
I am no longer a constant
But a question mark

Anxiety

My heart palpitates
A disturbing sensation
Uncomfortable
My hands shake
Not again
I've been through this before
And I wait for it to pass
I refuse to cave
And return to the cardiologist
Heart monitors
And tests
I know it's stress
Self-induced
Bottled up
Anxiety
And so I clean
Scrub the kitchen
Even behind the garbage can
With a sponge
And hot soapy water
Removing drips and smears
From my pale green wall
I sweep
Dirt tracked in from summer fun
Chase cat-hair tumbleweeds
And wash the brown wood floor
Working out tension
Nervousness
Intensity
Until the room shines
And my demons
Fall asleep

And Cloudy Days Bring Rain

The heart of a poet
Lips of inadequacy
Tears of self-doubt
Sadness on the page
Bringing forth age-old pain
Muddling through the days
The broken haiku
Every syllable struggles
Unrelentingly

I Passed the Maple Tree This Morning

A bright red mourning shroud
Your grief at summer's passing
Falling gently to the ground
Like drops of blood
On a late October snow
Unseasonable and cruel

Sometimes

Sometimes the world
Is dark and brittle
And as I walk
Twigs snap
Trees crash
And the smell of ozone
Is tight in the air

This is the draft of a life with no chance of a rewrite.

Of Times Past

You drew me in
Self-confident
Charming
Arrogant
With strength
and intoxicating dominance

I was starved for affection,
Sought out attention
Played the game
Pursued
Fell back
And you dove in
To let me see
The man behind the mask

I fell hard for a fragile fantasy
That shattered
Into shards of reality
That rode in
On the back of a tornado

Of Times Past II

We traded songs
Instead of words
And when you left
I deleted my playlist

Tear-filled baby-blues
My fault
I will never be able
To put the two halves of your heart
Back together

Summer afternoon sadness
Yet you took that selfie
And posted it to Facebook
Where it resides

It breaks my heart
That I had to break yours
To survive

Ruin

It took only fifteen minutes of
Tornado
Or straight-line winds
Don't correct me again
The destruction was the same

Another Time, Another Place

Ironic how the cat shred
The corner of the calendar
Where I recorded our dates
As thoughtlessly
As you discarded them

Distractions

I wrote a little today
Between checking messages
And candy crush
Running errands
And looking for the noodle I dropped
Beside the microwave
But I wrote a little
Came up with three story ideas
Two new poems
Edited some
And read a book
Cleaned the cat boxes
And walked

I procrastinated a little bit today
Or maybe a lot
More than I should have
And waited for text messages
That didn't come
And a visit
That was put off
Again
But I picked up
Just in case

I started to write
A little
On my new laptop
That makes it too easy
To jump onto Facebook
And yet I've walked away from it
To leave behind the posts
Of all the fun you're having
Without me

These I Own

When people read my words
Slapped onto a page
Coordinated, edited, printed,
Some will believe them to be
Amazing, inspiring, heartfelt
And grab their friends –
Put my book in their hands
And rush to the cash register
Those friends will eagerly
Turn the pages
Excited to watch
Woven words of art
Whisk them away
To depths of feeling
Never known before
And they will scoff
Say it's uninspired
Boring
Simplistic rhetoric
Drivel
They may be correct
As writing is
An intensely personal
Act
It is my passion
And torment
I own these words
And I fight to get them onto paper
Before they eat me alive

Judgment

Life is like a hangnail most days
You stare at the cuticle, that little piece of skin poking up
Taunting you
And know you should just leave it alone
Cut it back
Not give in to the pressure, because you know what will happen
Until you do
A push to the side
Slide back
And now it won't lay down
Give up
It rises up against you, dares you
And you gently grasp it
Because now it will hurt every time something brushes against it
It really can't stay
You rationalize
A pull
Slow and careful
That stinging satisfaction
That feels so clean
Until it digs a little deeper
Cuts in
Bleeds
A wound now that you should have left alone
And an embarrassment as you glance around
To see who is judging
As you grab a Band-Aid
Because it's preferable to have an injury
Rather than self-inflicted damage
Because the world judges the anxiety it has caused

No Refuge

My son has no refuge
His guard was down
When Covid hit
As were all
But he being more sheltered
And naïve than most
A happy Friday
With Monday expectations
Of the bus at six
School at eight-thirty
And a steady routine
Heavy with structure
And attention
Direction
He was greeted instead
With six months of freedom
More like a prison
Of anxiety
And confusion
Online assignments
Useless for my boy
Who still had hours
Of stimming
Endless singing
Over and over
Fingers in constant motion
His drawing no longer a comfort
But a necessity
Even that being shoved aside
For pacing
My son has no refuge
And I don't know how
To help him traverse
This madness

Autism Sucks

Autism sucks
It makes you only want orange juice
In an orange cup
Or water from a clear plastic bottle
It makes you only eat beige foods
While your body craves fried chicken
Mashed potatoes
Green beans
Your mind says no
And you reach for pancakes
But only at school
At breakfast
Home is for orange mac and cheese
Goldfish crackers
Or the occasional Chips-A-Hoy cookie
The chocolate bits picked out
And it must be the right size
Autism sucks
It makes taking a walk a process
Instead of an enjoyment
The reading of every "Posted" sign
Repeated, word for word, before you see it
But then having to check to make sure the words are the same
It makes you hyper-focus on the minutia
Instead of seeing the grandeur in the trees
The texture in the rocks
The voices of the birds
And yet all these things inundate your senses
And you press your hands over your ears
Shield your eyes
Autism sucks
It makes you say nonsensical words
Odd sounds
Repeat bits of commercials
It makes you watch the clock

Until 9:45 pm
When everything must stop
So you can go to bed
Where you bounce
And talk to the walls
Because you can't sleep
Autism sucks
It makes you want to open all the presents
On Christmas morning
Just to color the wrapping paper
Before crumpling it
Stuffing it under the sofa
And moving on to the next piece
Autism sucks
It makes you touch things
And line up toy trucks
In unrelenting order
It makes you turn on the TV for cartoons
Not because you want them
But because it is time
It makes you rigid in desire
Rooted in routine
I imagine you internally battling for change
That terrifies you
Struggling to put thoughts into words
That don't work
Autism sucks
And yet you smile
Brighter than anyone I know
And laugh
With such pure joy
When we connect
With our word games
And I make eye contact
With your soul

But How?

I have interacted with ghosts
Spirits
Guides
And guardian angels
Enough to know
There is an afterlife
I don't fear death
But I do know
Deep within my heart
That I must live
One day longer
Than my youngest
As he will never understand
The day that comes
When Mommy is no longer
Here

My white picket fence life
Is made up of posts that don't quite match
With paint cracked and peeling, the occasional knot,
And the gate won't shut

But the wood is strong
And each piece is beautiful
And unique

Barb Shadow

Sometimes you don't feel alone until you glimpse the thing that would make you whole.

A new month
A page torn away
Fresh, clean
Empty
A new beginning
That may have started
Last night
Over coffee

17 Again

17 again
At 55
You make me
17 again
Full of need
Desire
And insecurities
Does he like me?
Will he text?
And when you do
My heart pounds
I settle into the couch
Smiling at my phone
You've made me
17 again

You can bring the handcuffs
But make sure you have the key
I've lived too long
With hands tied
And only recently broke free

I Can Breathe

My melancholy has gone
Lifted
The fight between blue skies
And grey cloud
Is over
Quiet war raged
With only one soldier
Against herself
Battling emptiness
A punch to the gut
When there's no fist.
It wraps your arms
Around your stomach
Gasping to bring in air
But can't take a breath.
No pain
Just an absence of oxygen
That deep unnamed longing
Is quiet now
As I hungrily fill my lungs
With you

I Imagine

Sheets
cool and crisp
Like color-faded leaves residing under trees too long
And sun-bleached bones,
twigs from long broken branches
and aching hearts alone on February nights

Sheets
warm from the dryer
Like beach sand on a cloudless day
Wet bodies running from the ocean,
Wrapped in towels and sliding
Onto hot car seats

I rush to make the bed
And we dive in
Laughing as the heat dissipates
And I wrap my body with yours

From the Fire

I am reinventing myself
From deeper than the ground up
I will not be defined
By old relationships
And what was inflicted on me
I will trust the hell out of you
And not give in
To unfounded fears
I will walk the floor
Jaw tight
Knot in my gut
But I will not give in
And I will not give up
I will force my insecurities
Into submission
And I will win
Somehow
I will blink away the tears
That plague me
And ignore the red flags
That are innocent
Not indiscretions
I will be the phoenix
From his ashes
And I will fly with you

The Bridge Between

I walk between two worlds

One with no gravity
Where I take your hand
And touch the clouds

One where I am anchored
By an innocent soul
Who grips my hand
Like a lifeline

I hold them both
Show you the beauty
Of the earth
And teach my little one
To soar

Here I Am

I can't edit my life
The way I revise my books
Tweak the past
Rewrite the memories
But here I am today
A culmination of the years
Not perfect
But knocking on your door
And loving
That you let me in

Take me by the wrist
And show me by the fire in your eyes
What happens next

My World

Overthinking
Over thought
Thought over
Mulled
Considered
Thought again
Again again again
Pondered
Consumed
Procrastinated
Ruminated
Rethought
Gone over
Over done
So tired
Lost in thought
Thoughts lost
Pushing, prying
Breaking free
Spinning
Churning
Convoluted maze
Ridiculous worries
Yet one sideways glance
From you
Calms my storm
And subdues me to a smile

Words

I don't know where I stand
And yet I do, all too well
I know what I feel from you
And what I feel around you
And then I hear words
That don't echo your heart
That don't portray your actions
Or how we are together
They drop to the floor around our feet
And sound like footsteps of days past

Unchained

I see the differences
Then and now
Controlled and free
How much I missed
And lost
Weak and insecure
I stayed with the familiar
Took the next step
Instead of the right one
And now
And
Now
No safety zone
Breaking through old walls
Becoming the phoenix
I always should have been

What Else Would a Writer Do?

I think I need to start a journal
Just of you
To chronicle our times together
So I can reassure myself
They happened

Are happening

Without a Safety Net

I'm going outside my comfort zone
Which is new for me
Controlled for so long
Cut off from life
And told to fear the world
But with you
I find myself
Taking more than baby steps
Going out on a limb
On a branch
Solid and strong
I swallow my fears
And take your outstretched hand

Among the Dying Violets

I've put you on my calendar
After meeting for coffee
And an evening at your place
But in permanent ink
Because I've learned
What's written in pencil
May also be erased

Barb Shadow

I feel painfully awkward
Is it obvious?
Listening to you
Is like breathing
But when I speak
My words tumble over each other
And my thoughts
Stutter

I want your breath in my lungs.

Barb Shadow

    I've got no claim on you
          No hold
         Yet my heart
     Is firmly in your grasp
       And if you squeeze
  I will bleed through your fingers

I'm not broken if you don't see the pieces.

Trust

I can feel you about to burst
Emotion tight within your chest
Locked between blood and bone
Inside a heart I'm trying hard to stitch together
I see it in your eyes
And I know you're longing to say
The words that hurt you most
Tore apart your world
Come back to haunt you
But I swear I won't shred you
With my bare hands
Or kiss you with lips
Laced with acid
I'll just lay my heart in your hands
And hope you can trust enough
To keep it alive

God, I want to dive in
And lose myself
In everything you
I want to say I love you
When you're holding me
With my head on your shoulder
But I bite my tongue
So you don't tread
On old wounds
And pull away
To keep your soul
Safe

Barb Shadow

I am beginning to taste the flavor of life
And, no, this is not a cookbook.

I pick my head up from your chest
You say, "I love you,"
And I whisper,
"I love you, too,"
Then turn and go back to sleep.

Morning comes
And I want to ask
If it happened
Or was just a dream

We start our day
And I leave it alone
Not wanting to hear
It was

Late Nights

I hate driving when I'm so tired
Forcing eyes wide
Windows open
Cold air blasting
Music blaring
And knowing none of this
Is a safe solution
So I've vowed
To never leave your house
With fewer than
Two hours sleep
But we know
That driving at 4:30 am
Isn't that different
From 2:30
I still get home
In time to put my son on the bus
And climb into bed
For an hour
Before heading out again
In the car with the bumper sticker
That says
I'd rather be ghost hunting
But I think we both know
I'd rather be in your arms

In All Things

There is a gleam in your eyes
When you kiss me
Words cross my mind
Not my lips
Because your past
Has left you fragile
But I know in my heart
This amounts to love
And there is poetry here

It's the Simple Things in Life…

We break barriers
You and I
Of time
Of space
And sound
We shatter expectations
Make sense
Of chaos
And sing songs
Of triumph
And adversity

Just Saying

I choose to be okay
Until I am not
I refuse to see
Every scenario
Of you leaving
While we're together
I choose to trust you
Without suspicion
To not judge you
Based on my past relationships
I choose to be my best self
Because you deserve no less

Barb Shadow

I Come Alive

Because I love his smile

I leave my element
        To watch him come alive in his
And am perfectly content

He is vibrant
        And I could watch him shine
A million times

He looks over to me
        And confidently beams
I'll stay all night

Because I love his smile

My Next Life

I used to joke
That in my next life
I would be a groupie
Following a band
With abandon
And I would
Love a man
With tattoos
And piercings
Let the music
Fuel me
His love
Guide me
And at every venue
Be with the band
Who knew
I would have
My next life
In one lifetime

A Crisp Fall Morning

I catch the scent of his cologne
On my sweatshirt
And pause

I wish every breath were an inhale

My Soul Exposed, Again

We laugh
The two of us
Especially when the anxiety runs high
Mocking horror movies
And chic flicks
Except the ones
Where the heart overcomes us
And we blink away tears
Pretending it didn't touch
The deepest parts of us
You scroll through the channels
To find it again
While I protest
I hate to cry at movies
You give in to what we call comedy
We laugh
At the horrible acting
In Pet Sematary
And the deaths
In Final Destination
Irreverent and ridiculous
We are
And look at each other
In mock astonishment
"Why are we so twisted?"
And smile
We have shared the worst of times
And the absolute best

I Will Not Be Contained

Lay me to rest
Scattered on the wind
Let rain
Wash me to the sea
Watch for me
Where cardinals sing
And wild roses
Grow free

Smiles fall like autumn leaves
And laughter fades to mist
Yet
If you look, there is a bloom
Among the dying violets

ABOUT THE AUTHOR

Barb Shadow is a writer, living with her family on the East Coast. While this is her first book of poetry, Barb has authored a series of horror novels. When not out investigating the paranormal, she can be found at her writer's desk, coffee in hand, dreaming up nightmares for her readers.

To find out more about Barb and get updates on her upcoming titles, visit **barbshadow.com**. There you can follow her blog on the paranormal and contact her with any comments or questions you have. She is always happy to connect with fans!

Barb can also be found on Facebook **@BarbsWriting** and Instagram at **barbshadowwrites**.

www.ingramcontent.com/pod-product-compliance
Lightning Source LLC
Chambersburg PA
CBHW051655040426
42446CB00009B/1144